I0803022

MILES PRESS

Indiana University South Bend Department of English

TRACEY EMIN'S TENT

42 Miles Press
Editor, David Dodd Lee

ISBN 978-1-7328511-2-2 (pbk. alk. paper)

For permission, required to reprint or broadcast more than several lines, write to:
42 Miles Press, Department of English, Indiana University South Bend
1700 Mishawaka Avenue, South Bend, IN 46615

http://42miles.wordpress.com

Art Direction: Nick Kuder, Design: Olivia Novak, Production: Paul Sizer
The Design Center, Frostic School Of Art, Western Michigan University.
Printing: McNaughton & Gunn, Inc.

TRACEY EMIN'S TENT

POEMS BY JAKE BAUER

CONTENTS

For Penny

THE METHOD ACTOR

When I was younger, I was confused
each winter when suddenly the world
was not green. I had been taught things
are what they are: *we call this a chair*
because it's a chair; we call this
a trillium because it's a trillium.
But when they said without doubt
that this is the world, even though
it was frigid and white
and sometimes we could not
even drive on what they still called roads,
it was obvious to me this was not
the world. And when they said you
are Godfrey, but then one day
I was a half-man, gawky
and whiskered, how could I
trust anything? At first,
I was ashamed. Then, thankfully,
the subsequent thought:
I could be the trillium.
So when I shivered in the wind
and in winter when I disappeared,
I was. And: I could be the chair—
some people sat on me, some
chucked me across the room
when they were mad, and
some decorated me with jewels. Then,
what always happens happened
to me, too— people wanted to pay me
because I had discovered something
true about existence. And I took
their money, though often
it was not money.

AUTOBIOGRAPHY

We are in love
at six o'clock on Saturday—
January 8th 1927.
At two o'clock
on Thursday the 5th
of September, 1935,
we are not in love.

CINDY SHERMAN'S FILM STILLS

How gray and grainish in here

How everyone

What projector in the brain clicks What project

or what clicks What unmade omelets to be put away in the bit of fridge in here

Why beach

why bed why government

building Why question

where everything happens in here Where

rooms are plants Which exile

Textile

Which story is a soirée

Who scaredish Who fieldish When alone in here

is not alone When what you get

depends

MODEL APARTMENT

In the model apartment, Charlotte
is reclining in the chaise.
Everything in the model apartment
is tidy and industrial, like a locomotive.
Titanium and long, clean glass.
The floor is made of glass so
our one chore is to scour our reflections.
Before they brought me here
I wore slippers outdoors.
I sat by the shore in my skivvies.
Do you know what,
I ask Charlotte, but she goes under
my words like a squid beneath waves.
Her head is turned away.
She is scraping under
her fingernails with a penknife.
Even though I am here
and Charlotte is here
and Stuart and Flip and Reginald
and Emmyanne are here,
we are each alone. Being alone
is a science you must perfect
through experimentation, they say
over the loudspeaker. You must
fill the beaker with it.

ROBERT MAPPLETHORPE'S FLOWERS

These precious darling dignitaries
are perfect. Perfect
and piercing enough
to gore a bull
in a fight you've never seen.
Perfect Poppy bleeding bloom. Prim
and prayer, perfect petals. Here's one
you've never told anybody:
A blossom walks into a bank.
Gimme all ya got, the flower says,
holding up her pistil.
Perfect pun.
Thing is, you believe
in the swoop and arch, the strain
and the lighting of perfection, believe
when we die there's nothing
but a bit of elegant banter
to be had with the earth.
Perfect day for a stroll
through the garden of Please
and Quiet. *I'm looking for things*
I've never seen. Perfect
Orchid. Perfect
Magnolia.
I'm sorry, Mum.

BLIGHT OF THE JUNIPER

The room was filled with general impulses.

With some difficulty, Gillian reset the blown fuse in her imagination.

I, too, was feeling around in the dark corner for a bright thought.

I foamed iridescently like an outdated dishwasher.

Breakfast sausage would be served into the usual mouths.

A shy hiccup echoed down the tiled hall.

The only—*ah-hem*—symbolism is a doorway.

It walks us home from the party where everyone else is a lawyer.

HISTORY

In the world before this one, the first story was
Axe, how it told the sharp edge of itself
through the sandalwood. Sleep well, the tree said
as it tumbled into the gorge.

In the morning, the woman
loosens the day, slips
her foot in, and after
a deep breath, knots it
like a shoelace. Because of this,
what happens to her
happens to everyone,
she knows. And still,
she must use her toe
to squash the gnat crawling
across her kitchen floor.
She must earn herself
a splinter balancing
barefoot on the stepladder
in the shed. She must
walk to the park to meet
Selena who will whisper
something hurtful
romantically in her ear
and, after she leaves,
she must do some
calisthenics by the fountain
to clear her mind.

THE MINIMALIST

wants nothing more
than to be the aphid
chewing the leaf
Or better he thinks
as he looks out
his studio window
to be the ant that eats
the aphid The grouse
the snail the coyote
that eats the ant
His sister once
told him ants can
deconstruct a whole
house if neglected
He'd like to be
that house Maybe
his childhood
home Or why not
go further and be
the home inside
that home he says
to himself as he
wanders through
the front door
of his brain Why
not be its greenish
wallpaper

OYGBIV

Red featherbed said dread bred lead thread

Hereditary cherries in the incredulous orchard
slam into boyhood

Godhead zinnia

There's many a—   STOP

DO NOT ENTER

Recentered

Dredged heart slips dead over heels
for lady
bug in Miss
Scarlet's credenza

            There's tens a
red voices
inside your red choices

Seems
sacred   (hatred

confiscated)

Red of the early
enamored

A nail is not a person
until it is hammered

SECRET CABINET

When she is sad,
she opens
the mirrored door
of his mouth
and places inside
a trinket. Now
he speaks opal
heirlooms at the swim
club, pebbles
naturally heart-
shaped to strangers
in the town
gazebo. Five
minutes into their
anniversary dinner
she pulls him
to the bathroom.
She needs
to put a worry
inside of him
that is too big
to fit. Fate
occasionally comes
in a gorgeously-
bowed box,
done up
in floral print.
Seated on his
tongue is a Polaroid
of her tongue.
And when
she is happy—
O!—she keeps
his mouth shut.

MIRACLE WHIP

We borrowed the city under the waterfall.

The risk of smiling was the risk of attracting land-mice.

Cleaning supplies were called for.

Citizens tacked up lamplight in their dens.

Together, we had a turtle factory.

Had a wish.

We had a tight-knit government on stools.

We posed them outside so we could look through the window at them.

Haute couture was the needle skipping across the record.

THIS HAND IS A MAP

Hello lace dress Hello
marionette, "not yet—"   Say,
this line means no rest,
sure bet, pinky
to Bay
City. Ionia, anointed.

Detroited.

                                        Kalamawho?

There's a forest here. Boy forgotten
at daycare, wandering
the fate line: *I'm*   *I'm*   *I'm*
I'm   *I'm*   —

                                        White pine
                                                and white tailed
dear.

CHILD PRODIGY

One day I gave him paints and scrap paper so we would have
some finger-doodles for the fridge and when it was our turn to host
the spring croquet league my husband could boast, All originals
by Mr. Child Prodigy in the playpen. After, we were surprised,
but it was nice of Linda to invite over her friends from those New
York galleries. We had a few of my famous rosemary Pimm's
on the patio. And when they said his pictures were like a neo-Gorky
moonlighting as Mehretu, I just smiled— anyone want another?
No one could have turned down that first check—forty-seven
thousand!—but soon they started to read his work biographically.
When they intuited the wobbling of his parents' marriage,
how his baby sister was refusing to be conceived, he cocooned
in his insecurities: wouldn't leave our closet for entire days,
coated his body in white, rolled around on canvas, and responded
only to "Captain Ghost." The reviews, though, were rave.
Even after the divorce, more checks, but still he was only
eating bananas and getting in trouble at daycare after he learned
the word fuck shockingly quickly. So I took away his paints.
It was the only choice a mother had. He tried committing to
sculpture and installation, but, no, the critics were not pleased.
His thin body was all shaky. Then, when I discovered his final
painting, an image of the silence our voices speak into the wind,
done in our dog's blood, it was remarkable. Stunning. Staring
out his window, the world, then, seemed odd, like someone had
brushed it in green and silver, like there was a voice from far
away saying Gimme Gimme Gimme Gimme Gimme Gimme.

ENTARTETE KUNST

Into the measureless book,
without knowing anything
different, at the first
light on the first day
of their time on this shining earth,
they signed (even then,
painted?)
their names

*

                    Like everyone
you ever loved

standing
in a winter field making love

standing up, not touching:
impossible

to see   crack and char
in the museum
in your imagination   with your eyes

NEW BRAIN

I had promised myself I was done
combing these trees, yet here I am
among the poplars, again. I've studied
the old masters, memorized especially
the 8MMs, the screen prints
(arthropods circling a hurt bee,
cattail villagers). This must
be the forest. A girl up at the college told me
she'd seen an elk dancing modern, once.
So I've camouflaged my body,
pocketed my knife, my lust,
my notepad. I'm surviving
on exceptional mosses. My partner
fled, but soon I will spy them,
the masters, some standing, some
cross-legged, all working to sculpt
a new brain out of nature's fancy
symbols. I'll slip in, quietly,
like needlepoint, and inside
the new brain, the world will be lit
as if through stained glass.
Down the hall, a forest steps
from the bath. It dries the emerald
of its skin. It is clean. It is clean.
It works forty hours a week.
It goes to the store to buy cranberry yogurt.

SCARED OF THE VILLAGE

Down the hall, the couple is performing
the bedroom scene— mostly
instructional: how babies are made,
double lasso, and so forth. The one we are watching
is the foyer scene. The man plays
the role of the Man, putting on his cap
with the same foolish fortitude
he might any other night of his life.
In the kitchen scene, the couple kiss quickly over
tiramisu. They discuss city tax
code and recreational bird hunting.
The woman in the bathroom scene
is performing the role of Woman, Alone.
Splashing her face with water.
The play is called *Scared of the Village*.
At a predetermined instant, each version
of the couple will meet
in the den. They will walk in
and out of each other like specters, but we'll not
be there to see it. We are watching
the foyer scene, in which it is possible
to vacate the premises. The lighting
is bright. I squeeze your hand so it feels
like the word sorry. You're going
to love this, the Woman says
to her raincoat as she slips one arm in.

WHAT WAS RIDDEN IN WAS RIDDEN IN

Couldn't even toss my good name into a bucket on the beach.

I found myself a hummingbird.

I founded a hamlet in the valley of my quietude.

Good neighbors Mabel and Stanwick used to invite me over for rugby.

Brooke and Karina washed Ambrosia

in smoke in front of the inn.

I lay on the river. Beige grass was fit around me.

What is good is to return to where-is-required-of-you

is our hamlet's slogan. There is a door in the valley but

when there is a door in fear,

slide through it. If it is a puddle, lap from it.

WILL CASSIDY?

She's a spy
in a '60s blizzard
of song. Her pointed fingers hold the entire
whisper of capitalism on the head
of a match she has just struck.
A doctor resuscitates
the geraniums
she sees when she looks
through the window to the garden
of her mind. A child
happens there, swinging
over the milk vines
on a plank tied to a high branch.
How being quiet is a kind of career.

PENCIL SKETCH

Before I can learn to love you
I've got to finish this
intricate design I'm penciling
in the corner of the napkin
under my coffee. At first
when you asked how
we should spend our lives
together, a smoky pinkishness
radiated from the baseboard heaters.
Sometimes this also happens
to me when I eat red fruits.
Not easy to describe this
sketch: part maze, part
landscape, part fever
dream, Art Nouveau, Post-
Expressionism, Fluxus,
Constructivism, Deconstructivism,
Pre-Raphaelite. Breakfast is over.
You are arranging boxes
of things inside other boxes.
You are glowing, haloed. I want
to tell you you could be the most
famous architect; you could
ride a prize-winning horse
up the beach; you could
easily perform miracles
in a working-class town—a quiet
town where folk wear
their ambivalence warm,
like apricot tea, where
courting's still easy
on the eyelids—but there's
a lot of work to be done,
a whole mess of marks to get
organized in the corner here.

CAROUSEL

Wearing matching wool hats,
the couple drinks tea
from the smallest
ceramic mugs you've seen
this side of Impossible.
The mother ties balloons to the Eames chair.
The band leader
carves spoons
out of our laughter.
Every ceiling is a morgue
uncountable pigeons
might fall from.
One kind of shudder:
so fresh. And then
there's the other stuff,
old and stylish
and that particular hue
you usually only see
on snakeskin boots
and historic documents.
We've traveled daringly
to live in this glass box,
where the hand-carved horse
had to be put down.
It's Elia's job to press
the stop button
every three minutes.
Elia performs her duty
with a cozy
significance. Indeed,
Elia likes the word *ostensible*.
As in, a museum
of rocks. Their silence
the relief you've come to need.

CLASSICAL MUSIC

Thank you, quaintness.
Thank you, thumb-sized
harbor. Thank you,
pillowlight
of Denmark. I put my head
onto you.
I roll down
the low hill with you.
There are fake plants
I love. The weather
feeling more
like a bent
weathervane.

MACHINE

I'd been all morning
trying to fix this
damn thing. I was aiming
to finally nail down
the symbolic.
The field by the airport
walked right into me.
Someone was supposed
to mind the landscaping,
but now it's just all
overgrown in my gut.
Sometimes Meryl says
I need to shut off
the machine I use
for generating lies. Meryl
has these nice fingerprints
that remind me of ten
penguins in a desert.
But there really is
a certain kind of eyehook
you can use to attach
paradise to any working
memory. If my father,
who is made of rain,
ever phones me again
I'll head straight
out this window
and stand in the air.

THE COLLAGIST

The woods are
not a safe place
for a triangle,

but the triangle
can only travel
in one direction,

which is out, so
it exits the cabin.
The triangle does

not have unrealistic
fantasies. It knows
it is half a square.

So many
willowy shapes
in these woods,

I don't suppose
the earth is
interested

in making a lover
of me, it thinks.
But the creek,

of course, has
unexpected
desires. I'd let

you drink your
fill of me. You
could float down

me to the dappled
meadow where
I pool. No,

the triangle doesn't
trust in so much
color. What?

A kaleidoscopic
life? It curls
up on a stump

to doze. And—
Gotcha!—waking
inside the hunter's

thick mesh net,
the triangle
thinks of its

mother, the
Isosceles. How
lucky she is

not to have lived
to see her
only child *pasted*,

the hunter's voice,
as if from far
away, is washing

into the triangle's
brain, *beside the cut-*
out groom.

CELEBRATION

. . . And look! On your right is the children's pageant for adults. Gold.
It's translucent. It's colored-in. It's what is lost. Gold. You may Gold
notice Gold there are no children present. Raise your hand if you can
hear that God-crinkle of faux-cellophane from on your left: Gold saffron
gift-heart. Some of you will Gold want to visit the gift shop
for a travel-sized Gold tourniquet version— later. We are now
crossing the one hundred years of dust. The sun is hot. Up ahead, Gold Gold Gold Gold
balloon dog, looking rather acid-test-green in this light, says, First place!
Says, Joie de vivre! Says
I HATE YOU, JEF KONS.
Oh, yes, I am
happy to be here. Thank you for asking. My mother is quite well,
after all. Please, sir: pay attention. This is the spectacle
festival and I see you have all chosen to wear your
mouths, polka-dot scarves, and party hats— must each
thing mean? They say
when night temperatures in the desert reach subzero,
the best chance for survival is Gold
to gut an animal and climb inside.

ALL EVIDENCE TO THE CONTRARY

On her school-friend's
farm, the periodontist thinks
only of grapefruit. Pocket
watchless, righteousness
walks
away from her
like just another
dinner date
on a patio lined
with porcelain cups.
You can rain into them
if you are made of cloud.
If you blow in
from the plains
while maybe,
for example,
I'm dusting
my boots at the mouth
of our cavern.
Every word it whispers
is a wave
in your hair.
Salt. Eyelid. Agile.
They repeat themselves
while you are sleeping
over our bedspread.

WHAT HAPPENED TO GALY?

She wore good yellow.
She moved with weak eyes
to California after the capitalized
War. What happened to whom?
Her hair quilted into the festivities.
Ferociously, decorous
game demurred
with their wings.
Her back was straight.
Her granddaughter was married.
Wanting and not wanting *always*
wrestled on the thousand-foot lawn.
No one had hired a minister.
Shh. Listen— Propriety
was the diagnosis.

SONNET AFTER ANALYTICAL DRAWINGS AFTER PHOTOGRAPHS OF GRET PALUCCA

It *is* her! How X
makes the spot. Once

traced, troublesome
for the mind (wanting

and not, delighted
and not) to untrace:

simple insistence
there is no art

of the body—*the night*
you didn't tell me

you didn't love me
anymore, lightning, like

a hand, undid the elm,
remember?—but

THE CLOCKMAKER'S STORY

When he finally kissed her,
he became a banker
making complicated
exchanges in the currency
of affection. Before that,
he walked dogs professionally.
Before that, he had been,
for a short time, in the circus
and when he dipped his head
in the lion's mouth, it was
the crowd who roared.
But now, at her door
in the drizzle, *just one*
more, just one more—
he became a Ferris wheel.
He became a paleontologist.
He became the shawl
Nana knit. How amazing,
she thought, massaging
the thin fabric with her fingertips.
It felt like a shawl made
of Courage. Pulling it
over her mouth to protect
herself from the wind,
she thought, I will wear this
to the Governor's funeral.
I'll go ice climbing in strange
fjords. What was sharp
inside her coiled like a—
whaddayacallit—
Slinky. She wiped her glasses
with the corner of her shawl.
I will build myself
a very private bomb shelter.

THE MINIATURIST

carved miniature sculptures of giants: *Immaculate*, yes, *Performed with the utmost precision*, yes. And, of course, he could admit his giants were exactly the same size as a human, but *Perfect realism? —— The ultimate expression of personhood? ——* No; no; no; no, he raged. Just consider the jawbone's circumscription of the mouth, the spindling metacarpals— no human could exhibit such poise. By reducing what is more mammoth than life to the mere size of life, there could be no death, he thought. He would show them.

So that evening the crowd discovered in his studio window a thing smaller than anything they had ever witnessed— so grotesque in its tininess they tried to shove their human fists into their eye sockets, but it was already too late, and that was the end of everything, the child's mother said.

But what's in the window, the boy asked. So careful in his smallness, she thought, and with words bigger than her mouth could hold she said, Maybe tomorrow, my little giant, your father and I will take you into town to see. Turning off the light and kissing his cheek, she said, Maybe tomorrow, and, Sweet night.

PROPHET

The Time Woman lives on the old playground up Rifle Range Rd.
Behind the abandoned chapel. Up there,
I've seen people get five years younger.
I've seen the moon rise twice in a minute.
Maybe I haven't used every retry
like I meant to. *O,*
could I shield thee from every harsh wind.
No, we are not a town who appreciates time
tadpoling around like a whirlpool
in the kiddie pool.
But about reading the hours
in the play equipment? Fifty years from now
I am the Time Woman's grandmother
teaching her mother who will soon
teach her. An eagle
strung up from the swing set.
Two hands that are bears.
To buy groceries,
I sell fresh fish and berries
to tourists arriving on the Summer Resort Line—
isn't a winter line.

CY TWOMBLY DANCE PARTY

This trout farm used to be a super

highway.

This red snowsuit articulates itself in the lawn.

I don't want to miss a second of the trombone solo.

There were houses on the hand towel—

drawings of houses.

The steamship carried fascination to our squirrely legs.

More or less the catatonic sound of a slipper.

The mismanagement of an orchard

by a troupe of nice enough actors from down south.

SPIRAL

The half a lemon
in my head gets squeezed
into the steaming mug
in yours, and suddenly
we are both imagining
the same soirée.
All red décor.
All sequined suits.
Strawberries served
with cute chocolate hats
in the hallway,
and when nobody
wants to watch me
spin like a clock hand
on the faux-brick
exterior, I say
That's fine. I snap
some more Polaroids.
Dahlia rose bushes
in the garden. Double Dutch
on the driveway?
Okay.

Would you hand me that
woolen blanket? Could you damage
my bottle of suntan oil? By burning
it? Or gently sailing it into the ocean?

I SINK IN THE SINK LIKE A THIMBLE

I know a ship and
a miniature goose
on a ship.
I know a sweet way
to say *harness*.
My karaoke club
disbanded, so most
evenings I visit
my neighbor, the goat
collector. Not farmer,
for his love of animals
is precise, but far
from what you'd call
rustic. I want you
to know what I felt
for you really was
like that. A real
polished bullet
(ca. 1910) to set
in the glass case
in the hallway
beside my collection
of household replicas:
a papier-mâché first
aid kit, a clay Dawn
bottle. From the

moon-side, every
version of myself
arrives to kick
down my front door.
Do we know
which are good
and which are evil?
Do we know what
keeps mastication
from rising
to the most popular
team sport? No.
No, we do not.

CLOUD TALKS TO TREE

Cloud has big friends.
Tree naps in its own deer blind.

What you thought

you wanted was
an idea.

Some morsel for the mouth.

    I'm not even hungry; I just don't want pleasure
to end.

ARBOR DAY

The pool of miracles
you get to drink
from at birth only
made Sima thirstier.
She wanted to down
that unexpectedly
sultry look the two
strangers shared
at the planetarium.
She wanted to bathe
in the cautious
thoughts lifeguards
must have on their
ways home. She
announced to the
bowl of raspberries,
I am definitely
unsatisfied just licking
your condensation.
Nevertheless, thanks
for being the liquid
you are, she thought,
as she popped one
into her mouth,
wishing it was hotter,
like the miracle
she knew she'd
always hoped
to swallow. Like
a high fever. Or
perhaps, actually,

more like a volcano,
she thought. She
had, once, after
taking a plane, a boat,
and a bus, ridden
a bike seven miles
to try to drink one.
It turned out to be
a small, dumpy thing,
not even worth a sip.
The only other
visitor was a little
boy who was playing
with a broken yoyo.
Sima left in tears—
rode the bike, the bus,
the boat, the plane.
When she got home,
she found a tiny
grave dug in her
front yard. Only big
enough for an insect,
really. She put a
penny in it. She put
in some rock music.
She lied to it and
said she was a tender
of orchards, a drinker
of apricot tea, a dancer,
a time machine,
a clockmaker. But

the tiny grave could see the truth. It said things back to her like *Fear is nature's artificial flavoring* and other gibberish it had heard other holes say to other humans. Those other humans had always eventually wandered off, but not Sima. She sat down in the damp grass with her back against a stump. She crossed her legs at the ankles. Without really thinking about it, she licked her thumb.

THE MACHINE THAT APPLIED THE PRESSURE

was bought from a woman
in Watersmeet. The pressure
was sometimes
like grabbing minnows
with her grandfather, other times
like pushing an owl
through a tear in some fabric
hung from the clothesline.
The woman's existence
was the narrow hall
of the one-room library
in that town. The yellows
of it. The lilac and alabaster.
The wise old owl, the more
he knows, the less he says,
he reminded himself
as he watched the woman
under the jack pines
using her hands to talk
to lovers, sometimes lying
them flat like rapids
on the Ontonagon River,
sometimes making them
judder like a camera, which,
not too long before
had been invented,
and, by pressing down,
also captured silent things.

WEDDING

How wonderful. Everyone who was supposed to
got married. As I sat there in what I had believed
to be a fairly accomplished outfit, beyond the copse
a goat led a blind horse through the bramble
to pasture. The sun set and rose at an unexplainable
pace, and each day they did it again— those two
unlikely companions, one wanting to eat, the other
to be relied upon. My own friends said their vows
once, with triumph, then went on to married life,
cheated on one another several times, divorced,
remarried...the woman first, then the man, I heard.
I never did believe in them, though I loved each one
with pain. Nights, the goat led the horse back to her
favorite patch of dirt, until one morning she passed
noiselessly. Two days later, the goat as well, and,
smoothing my rumpled clothes, I exited that special
occasion no older than on the afternoon I had arrived.

THE QUEEN

So small she often perches
upon the lap of the miniature statue
of herself seated in her miniature,
etched throne. Sometimes,
with her scepter and mouse-skin
robes, she wanders into town,
nearly forgotten. Her rule
was long ago vast and unyielding.
But recently she has loved only
to enter the depot or general store
and, in the corner, perform
her one-act play—
a catalog of modest misfortunes:
the dropped thimble, etc.
No who to declare war on, taxes,
or when to release the guillotine—
just the unmade bed, misplaced
spectacles. Then she bows
to the empty chairs.
These days (forbidden to leave),
I am the only one who remains
in the castle. I bathe the ivory
statue. I polish the brow
and scowling lips. I do not dare
inquire if she loves me—
one does not ask the queen
questions like this.

WILL RON EVER IMPROVE HIS ROCK GARDEN?

is an example of the kind of question I am.
At least, that's the theory
Harriet shies toward. Where is the safe?
is another example, I realize
when Harriet asks for the third time
at the outdoor table at the clam shack
while we are re-christening
our alliance. It's a theory
that when you step into it
has the aura of a plush minivan,
Harriet explains. Then she sips
her strawberry-lemon soda.
She chews with the same style
I have observed librarians chewing.
Very rapid jaw movement
once the food has arrived at the teeth.
The only place the minivan will drive you
is to the pawn shop, Harriet continues
now that she has swallowed her scallops.
She continues in a fashion
that makes you wonder if you are
actually on a zipline. The world
feels very far from your feet. My clams,
I can see without touching them,
are cooling down fast. Nearly
at light speed, it seems, but they are not
getting any closer to my mouth.
I know, I know, I say with that mouth,
when you pull up to the pawn shop,
do not thank the driver. Just exit
the vehicle, walk inside, and purchase

the golden watch— real cool and
nonchalant-like, but also with
a convincing air of confidence, I say,
barreling through the instructions.
Harriet cranes across the table
to position her mouth right beside
my ear. What the fuck are you
talking about, she says, annunciating
the words as if they were floating
lily pads and she the solemn frog
hopping from one to the next.

THE ORIGAMI ARTIST

When I woke that morning and there was no God anymore,
there was nowhere else to turn. I had a friend who'd
recommended her, I told her on the phone, because she'd cured
the distressingly evil look in his infant daughter's eyes.
She remembered his case, and, to my surprise, chuckled
at my joke—mispronouncing origami *oh-my-god-me*—
so she agreed to attempt the fold she had always wanted
but never had the chutzpah, she said, to attempt before:
the human spirit. But first, she would have to fold my life.
So in June, I received a paper creation of my grandmother
arm-wrestling my mother; in July, my mother filling
a beehive with cherries; August, my sister picking the lock
on the cage where we kept the ocean. I was moved
and impressed. Then, inside the last box: a paper gun.
I pointed it at the desk, at the fish tank, out the window
at the kids playing hopscotch, up in the attic, down
in the basement, at the kitchen table, the mantle,
the bookcase, and then into my mouth, and when I pulled
the paper trigger what burst from the back of my skull
hung in the air like chalk two dusty hands have clapped.

BROADCAST

Suddenly, the world is gigantic.
It has grown overnight.
You see this while you are eating cereal.
A very sugary cereal.
An unnatural berry flavor in it, for sure.
A bug crawls across the painted baseboard.
It is a centipede.
In fact, there are two of them,
which means this is a love story.
Maisie coughs.
Maisie shortens her bangs.
There is now something about them
that says "Hi, group,"
like she is standing in the middle
of a circle of chairs.
She says the way you are sitting gives off a feeling of spring.
A design feeling.
A downtown feeling.
A feeling feeling. A buck
walks by the window.
It is polishing its antlers on the bark of a tree,
and you think
We never had a window there before.

THE EXPLANATION

Until the inventor
made the man
into a periscope, the man
had never seen land.
He went inside
his encyclopedia
to find mountains.
The people who lived
in what he learned
to call foothills
created music
in their driveways.
He wanted to explore
that stuff
inside of them.
He wanted to find out
what *noble* meant. But no,
definitely no
fucking way,
the inventor said. He was
an ocean-dwelling instrument.
He already had
a noble calling:
espionage. And there
was that word again,
the man thought.
And then he thought,
I am an ice cube,
which the world

honestly believed
and so for him it poured
itself into a pint glass.
There were
forests there. There
were begonias,
yellow and pink
and red. And reclining
in her deck chair,
the inventor took a sip.

THE NEW PAINTING

The doctor rode the horse
into town. Or the horse riding
town into the doctor...

In the new painting by
[   ] a yellow
-speckled stool is stacked
(carefully) with
human skulls,
which we discuss over
crepes and malbec
in the garden.
                    Massacre
is the pinnacle
of mortal enterprise, you say,
touching your pointer finger
to mine. We have been married
twenty-seven years
too long.
            The horror,
I say, of the labor class is
they are a mystic...
Then the teleprompter shuts off.
We wriggle out
of our tight suitcoats,
quick.

When we woke all the trees
were made of gold

I WAS THE MOON

Especially because
I never saw the moon,
I was ready
for Kristiana. Kristiana
Fisticuffs; Kristiana Wrench
and Silly String
I called her
from the moon.
I was the moon
she said
in reply and that's not
the last
I remember
of the emergency.
Imagine a cart
like Kristiana,
full up of real
warmth, traveling
the country
with an excess
of minds. Bright
fish stepped all over
my hands.

Pretty much
never even tasted porridge
until the morning
when rococo came over
to borrow
some human
nature. Kristiana
at the window
was petting a doe.
Because
I was the moon
I was ready
for Kristiana. Kristiana
who said a lot
of important words
on stage
in the basement
while I
was affecting the tides.
Who biked circles
around her treehouse
as if it were
whistling
like a tea kettle.
The sun rose for one hour.
Bright fish
stepped all over my hands.

ROYGIV

Blue grew through you

Tchotchke peacocks at the abandoned zoo

Around and around the blue cages, riding the children's train
toward *always*, eating gorgonzola

Choo choo

Blue under blue over blue

          Even aquamarine is possible at the State Hospital
(closed nineteen eighty-nine)

Ten thousand IT'S A BOY balloons
rubbing together make
the blue sound
of a hacksaw

Uranus   (death

is famous)

And oh, threnody, *beauty is therapy*

          . . . something new, something borrowed, something
thereunto

Blue
of the awesome, wet we've—

If you want what I've got you have to hold it
until you've imagined how to breathe

THE GERHARD RICHTER SCALE

This ocean
is not the ocean
I wanted

to take up
residence in your
handbasket

of easy crimes
little swipes
of golden

bikes, pre-dawn
I mean
I mean

she had a lot
to accomplish
with her feet

all day was
was only halfway

AMERICAN REALISM

Inching our hands
along each other's backs,
like wary caterpillars,
through the Good Thing
Gallery, we happen
upon a charcoal drawing
of a sculpture of a woman
looking at a photograph
of a toy theatre
in which a marionette
is looking at a charcoal
drawing of a
sculpture of a woman
looking at a   looking
at a   looking
at a
          Etta
James
in the background
singing "Your Good Thing
(Is About to End)"

PARTY

Mark gulped breast milk straight from the carton. Nice party,
Carolyn said to Franz, who was relishing cone after
cone of strawberry soft serve. Flecks of powdered
milk speckled her lips. On the balcony, Tomas and
Tomaž used miniature forks to feed each other cheesecake.
Bill sipped kefir through a straw. Afterward, a few guests tried
to hold Russell back as he continued to accost the piñata,
splattering quark across the endless linoleum floor. Eventually
he was pacified by 2% yogurt. Time stopped. Then she laughed
and milk came out of Maya's nose. Who wants to do shots,
Death asked, lining up ounces of crème fraîche on the mantle.
Still sucking his stick of butter, Philip said, I'd better not.
Everyone else lifted a glass—*Arriba, abajo, al centro, pa' dentro!*—
as the bell chimed again. Things are really getting wild now,
Maxine said through a mouthful of curds, opening the door
to find James on the porch, his hands cupping cottage cheese.
Behind him, earth was the color of condensed milk.

NOTICE TO EVACUATE

Your residence in Tracey Emin's tent is no longer permitted.
Tracey Emin's tent was lost in a fire.
There is no Tracey Emin's tent. You are living
in your head, that's all. Beatific, I'm sure,
with your desperation & longing,
but under present circumstances
it cannot be allowed. May I
be honest, though, Sir?
Sometimes I wish I were you.
The wind rakes the cheeks out here.
No Lesley. No Etiana. No Mrs. Matel.
No olive-fingered woman gave birth to a woman
who gave birth to me. Neither lay
me in the cot of her arms. None
later that were pornographic. None gentle.
None were like mice. Then the love
of my adult middle-class life never
rolled over and tried
to stab me in the thigh with a pair of scissors.
Not one best friend flying over the ocean
let me with a pillow
against his shoulder. And in that warm, cramped space
he did not also rest his
on the crown of my own.

LETTER FOUND UNSENT

Dear Your Royal Highness—
                                                  You may already be informed, cozy
in your palace of finches, but I want to be clear: Surrealism
has no life left in its haunches. We have taken
the coastline and the scraggly hills. Ta-da, we have it surrounded.
You were right, the loons here do simper like magi. And when you said
want is greater than any need—
you crafted a kingdom from that. Often, this escapade
has reminded me— when you were a young woman you lusted
after two brothers, one a dogwood, the other a snow
rose bonsai. I can only imagine
how distinct each bonfire. As a boy, I watched from the creek bed
as the next day the men dismantled the circus tent. The fragile
but emotionally generous vole you abandoned in the trenches even
now is speaking of his affection for you. It is not too late
to sign the accord.

TWO-DOLLAR MAZE, CHARITY

Her lover's hair
was a cornfield! She found it

rippling on the pillow.
A tightrope

an ant might walk.
If it had to get daringly

from here to there.
I'll story in the wings.

I'll never get fresh.
Look! a wall

made of clouds.
You could fall asleep

in the shower
and wake up. Lying

in a field of rain the color
of skin coating you.

NOTES

13 Robert Mapplethorpe spoke the italicized words in an interview with *ArtNews* in 1988

23 "Entartete Kunst," translated as Degenerate Art, shares its title with the 1937 Nazi exhibition of the same name

35 "Celebration" shares its name with the series of sculptures by Jeff Koons and takes place at the Metropolitan Museum of Arts' exhibition "Jeff Koons on the Roof" in 2008

41 "Prophet" is inspired by Isamu Noguchi and the quote is taken from "Founding a Tent-Home in California," originally published in *National Magazine*, Volume 23, by Léonie Gilmour, Isamu Noguchi's mother

66 "Party" is dedicated to the many poets we lost between February 2014 – July 2015

ACKNOWLEDGMENTS

I am grateful to the journals where the following poems, or earlier versions, were first published:

The Queen: *Bateau*
The Collagist: *The Chattahoochee Review*
Celebration: *DIAGRAM*
Robert Mapplethorpe's Flowers; Secret Cabinet: *Elke*
The Origami Artist: *Enizagam*
Notice to Evacuate: *Forklift, Ohio*
R O Y G I V: *Foundry*
Broadcast; The Explanation; The New Painting; I Was the Moon: *The Glacier*
This Hand Is a Map; Entartete Kunst: *Inter/rupture*
Cloud Talks to Tree; Arbor Day; Will Ron Ever Improve His Rock Garden?: *The Laurel Review*
Pencil Sketch: *Mudfish*
Wedding: *Pacifica Literary Review*
Machine: *Phoebe*
American Realism: *Poetry Northwest*
Child Prodigy: *Public Pool*
O Y G B I V; The Gerhard Richter Scale: *Puerto del Sol*
The Machine that Applied the Pressure: *RHINO*
Model Apartment: *Spillway*
New Brain: *Third Coast*
The Method Actor: *The Threepenny Review*
Sonnet After Analytical Drawings After Photographs of Gret Palucca: *Thrush Poetry Journal*
Two Dollar Maze, Charity: *Timber*
Party: *Two Peach*
Blight of the Juniper: *TYPO*
Scared of the Village: *Up North Lit*

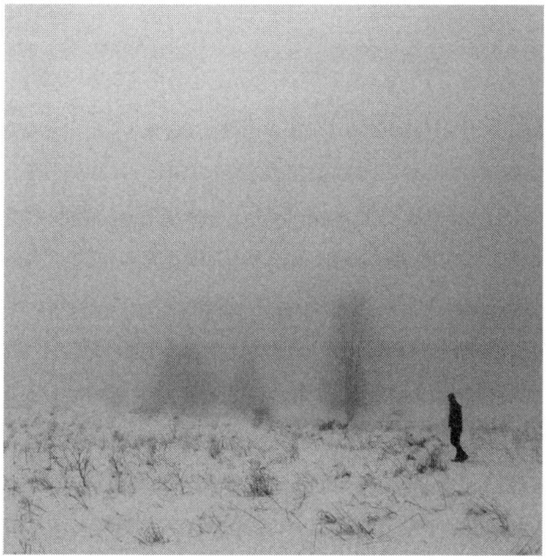

Jake Bauer is the author of the chapbook *Big Pool, Oh* and co-author of the chapbook *Idaho Falls*. He lives in Traverse City, MI.